Color Library Travel Series

ENGLAND

Designed and Produced by
Ted Smart & David Gibbon

MAYFLOWER BOOKS · NEW YORK CITY

erse, exciting and steeped in
ory, London's magic
tinues to enthrall all who visit
lovely city. *Above far left:*
ckingham Palace; *near left* the
usehold Cavalry along the
l; *below far left* Her Majesty
Queen taking the salute at the
ooping the Color Ceremony';
w *near left* footguards of the
usehold Brigade; *above* the
Edward's Crown; *below* St.
l's Cathedral; *above right*
uses of Parliament beyond
nbeth Bridge, and *below right*
cadilly Circus.

Polperro, one of Cornwall's many attractive villages, is pictured *above and left; below* Norman tower of Tewkesbu *right* the ruins of Glastonbury Abbey, Somerset, and *above* the sleepy village of Upper Slaughter in the Cotswolds.

own *above left* is Saddlers Mill
he old market town of
msey in the New Forest; *left*
uresque cottages at Charlton
he Vale of Evesham; *above*
tle Combe in Wiltshire; *right*
an Green in Hampshire, and
ow the carved hillside figure –
Osmington Man – near
ymouth.

...ng the popular attractions
... south coast are
...ourne *above left;*
...ton, with its famous
... *left;* Beachy Head *top*
...s lighthouse *center right,*
...irling Gap *top right.*
...ificent Man o' War Bay,
...f Lulworth, can be seen
... *right,* and *below* The
... Man of Wilmington,
...ed to be of Saxon origin.

Scotney Old Castle, near Lamberhurst *right,* the weatherboarded mill at Farningham *below,* and the pretty village of Chilham *above* are sited in the county of Kent. Eastbourne's regal esplanade is shown *above right,* and *left,* delightful Rye in Sussex.

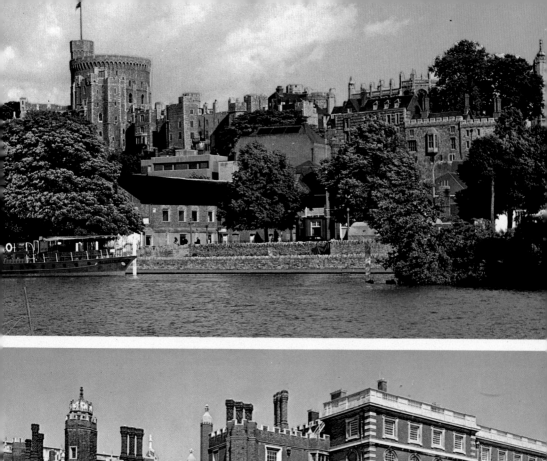

Windsor Castle, the Queen's Berkshire home is pictured *left;* *above* famous Eton College, Berkshire, and *below left* historic Hampton Court. All Souls College *below,* St. John's College *top right,* Nuffield College *center right* and St. Edmund Hall *bottom right* are part of the country's famed Oxford University.

Stately Blenheim Palace, Oxfordshire, ca be seen *above; left* the old mill at Hambleden, Buckinghamshire; *below* Henley on Thames and its regatta course *right,* in the Thames Valley, and *above righ* Finchingfield, Essex.

Norfolk, famous for its waterways – the Broads – where Horning *above* is a noted touring center, also offers many interests, including Great Yarmouth' model village *below*. Cavendish *left* and Kersey *bottom left* are two of Suffoll prettiest villages, while *righ* can be seen the Gothic spir of Canterbury Cathedral in Kent.

Cambridgeshire, site of the
American Cemetery *bottom
left,* is noted for Cambridge
University set on the banks of
the River Cam *right.* Among
its halls of learning are King's
College *above,* Christ's Colleg
center left and Trinity College
with its clock tower *below* and
'Nevilles Court' *top left.*

Stratford-upon-Avon, with its Ho
Trinity Church *below,* Anne
Hathaway's Cottage at Shottery
above right and Royal Shakespear
Theater *right* is renowned as the
birthplace of William Shakespea
Left is shown imposing Compton
Wynyates, Warwickshire, and
above the delightful Willy Lott's
Cottage, Flatford Mill, Suffolk.

Shown *left* is the superb 17th century garden of yew trees at Packwood House, Warwickshire; *above* charming Bridge End, Warwick; *below* magnificent Chatsworth House in Derbyshire, and *right* the Grand Union Canal and Lock at Braunston, Northamptonshire.

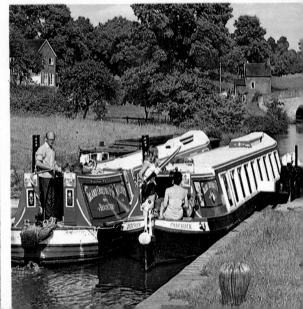

e examples of Cheshire's half-
ed architecture are evidenced in
Moreton Hall *left,* Bramall Hall
and at the Cross in Chester *right.*
below is the tower of Chester's
sandstone cathedral.

Seen *left* during the ann
illuminations, Blackpoo
Tower *below* dominates
popular resort on
England's north-west c
Shown *above and right* is
dockland area of Liverp
an important seaport in
Merseyside.

Yorkshire's fascinating and diver
scenery is evidenced in Bolton
Abbey *above;* Whitby *right;* Riev
Abbey *center left,* and Muker *bott
left.* Snow-sprinkled Troutbeck i
the Lake District is pictured *top*
below Lindisfarne Castle, Holy
Island, Northumberland, and *rig*
a view of the bridges spanning th
river at Newcastle-upon-Tyne.

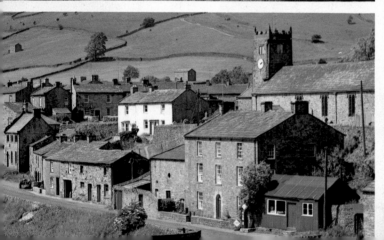